Rebuilding Families After Abuse

Rebuilding Families After Abuse

Papers from a conference at the National Children's Bureau

Edited by
Anne Hollows

Brian Hutchinson
Child Protection Multi-Agency Training Co-ordinator

The National Children's Bureau was established as a registered charity in 1963. Our purpose is to identify and promote the interests of all children and young people and to improve their status in a diverse society.

We work closely with professionals and policy makers to improve the lives of all children but especially young children, those affected by family instability, children with special needs or disabilities and those suffering the effects of poverty and deprivation.

We collect and disseminate information about children and promote good practice in children's services through research, policy and practice development, publications, seminars, training and an extensive library and information service.

The Bureau works in partnership with Children in Wales and Children in Scotland.

© National Children's Bureau, 1995

All rights reserved. No part of this publication may be reproduced, stored in a retrieval system or transmitted in any form or by any person without the written permission of the publisher.

ISBN 1 874579 35 0

Published by the National Children's Bureau, 8 Wakley Street, London EC1V 7QE. Telephone 0171 843 6000. Registered charity number 258825

Typeset by Books Unlimited (Nottm), NG19 7QZ

Printed and bound in the United Kingdom by Biddles Ltd, Guildford

Contents

1 **Introduction**   1
 Anne Hollows
 Child Abuse Training Unit, National Children's Bureau

2 **An overview**   5
 Jenny Still
 The Faithful Foundation

3 **Issues for and about children**   16
 Abe Glaser
 Consultant Child Psychiatrist
 Guy's Hospital, London

4 **The offender's perspective**   20
 Dawn Fisher
 Forensic Clinical Psychologist
 Raeside clinic, Birmingham

5 **Issues for and about the non-abusing parent**   28
 Jacqui Sayers
 Social Worker, Child and Family Psychiatry, Bath

6 **Deciding to rebuild a family after sexual abuse**   37
 Margaret Adcock
 Social Work Teacher and Consultant

Appendix: The workshop session: the practitioners' challenge   46

References   50

1. Introduction

Anne Hollows, Child Abuse Training Unit
National Children's Bureau

An analysis of media coverage of child sexual abuse would be likely to demonstrate that, while the subject has regularly been a headline issue, attention has focused almost exclusively on investigation and detection. It has been difficult to attract the same level of interest to the processes which follow the detection of abuse. Public concerns have fuelled a similar preoccupation among professionals and while there is increasing professional acknowledgement that both victims and abusers need treatment, as yet there are few options available. Furthermore there is little clear evidence at present about the effectiveness of treatment, especially for abusers. What is known suggests that abusive behaviour is addictive, that recidivism among abusers is high, and that the effects of the abuser's grooming of victim and family to meet his needs will last long into the future.

So what are we to do when an abuser and his family want to rebuild their life together? How are we to ensure the safety of the children whose protection is our legal duty? Does the crime of sexual abuse of children demand a sentence which lasts far longer than that imposed by the criminal court: the virtual permanent separation of abuser from his own and, indeed, any other family? Or do we believe that family ties are so strong that the risk of abuse is of secondary importance when considering the chance of reconstructing a family?

The answers to these questions have implications for all families where sexual abuse has taken place. They have implications for the wider, community-based protection of children who may be at risk from abusers who have completed a prison sentence but who may not have changed at all. They have implications for the way we develop, manage and resource treatment, for both children and adults. They have implications for the notion of justice for those convicted of crimes of sexual abuse. And, if family ties are indeed more important than the risks of sexual violation within a family, then there are implications for the foundations and principles of our child protection system and for our understanding of, and commitment to, children's rights.

The chapters in this book, like the conference for which they were produced, offer an elaboration of the state of current professional thinking in this field. Drawn from a range of professionals in different settings, they seek to offer a perspective on the potential for rebuilding families for each of the key stakeholders: the child, and other children in the family; the mother, or non-abusing parent; and the abuser. These perspectives are prefaced by an overview in chapter 2 from Jenny Still, formerly of the Gracewell Clinic and now working at the Faithful Foundation. Her conference presentation included a dramatic video excerpt of abusers in treatment brainstorming their response to the word 'child'. Few of those who attended the conference will forget the clashing juxtaposition of our own earlier brainstormed response to the word innocent; pure; flower; perfect with that of the Gracewell residents. It proved an important device in helping us to face the realities of the distortions which permit child abuse to occur.

But to close our minds to the possibility of change is to deny, for most of us, our professional commitment to the possibility of change and our duty to act as agents of change within that process. What clearly has to be addressed is 'what needs to change?' if children are to be protected from an abuser living in the same house. This must be followed with key questions about how the change is to be accomplished and, critically, about the management of that process. One of the main focuses of the group discussions at the conference, reported in this book, was the issue of strategic management of intervention in abusing families. Next comes the maintenance of change, which is critical if reconstituted families are to avoid the additional trauma of continual close scrutiny. We must look too, in this context of multiple deceits, at the extent to which change may be a mirage: sometimes a consequence of our own desperate hope to see a positive outcome, but also a response to the current pressures to preserve family units and to work within tight budgets.

Abe Glaser's poignant presentation in chapter 3 of the issues affecting children points to the reality that children's responses to adults may be so ingrained that their own sense of choice, and ability to choose, is very limited. This brings another reality: that we are all forced to work with rebuilding families in situations where we may not feel that the child's interests are being served at all by the process. Dawn Fisher, in chapter 4, offers an overview of the research about the characteristics of abusers so that, in the midst of the competing demands which surround proposals for rebuilding families, there are some research-based certainties in our decision making. In chapter 5, Jacqui Sayers looks more optimistically at the potential for work with mothers, who are increasingly identified as the major factor in predicting outcome for a child. Her chapter approaches rebuilding by looking at the options for developing a gradual restoration of contact between abusers and child, always set in the context of the ability of the non-abusing parent to protect a child. She also looks at the potential of mothers to develop therapeutic, protective parenting.

Finally Margaret Adcock, who summed up the proceedings, has expanded her comments into a chapter which addresses the key issues upon which decision making will hinge for the professionals involved. She helpfully provides some examples of criteria for decision making which can be used not only within the professional arena, but also as tools for families to formulate their own codes of practice and behaviour.

The reports of the group sessions at the conference have been incorporated into an appendix describing the dilemmas common to the experience of practitioners who work in this field. This Appendix reflects not only the professional and practice issues raised by reconstituting families but also the impact upon a fragile area of practice of major shifts in management and structure within agencies.

Terminology in this area of work varies and words used to describe the process include reconstruction and rebuilding. The expression 'rebuilding families' seems, however, the most appropriate metaphor to describe the detailed work which should be undertaken with individuals and with family groups. The painstaking process of putting each part of the process in place is clearly crucial if the eventual outcome is to withstand uncertainties and overcome fear and hurt. It is certainly a process which cannot be rushed and one where a number of professionals play their part in working out a clear plan. So we have chosen, in this publication, to use the term rebuilding throughout the book.

The book offers a summary of key research as well as first hand accounts of practice and practical guidance. The context into which it falls is a difficult one, however, for all those who plan to work in this area. Resources for complex interventions with families are limited. There is a rising tide of moral pressure to preserve family units at (almost) all costs. There are voices, raised loudly, maintaining that sexual abuse is often an invention of children and social workers. Our enthusiasm to increase the provision for treatment of offenders implies that we believe a significant number of offenders attending for treatment can be changed, even cured, by the process.

The message of the chapters which follow suggests that we must rely upon the individual analysis of factors in each case. We must use the outcome of our analysis to ensure that practitioners, managers, and the judiciary in both criminal and civil cases, are clear about the issues, the choices and the risks. And we must continue to argue for the development of well supervised resources and skilled staff to develop good practice in this area of work. If rebuilding families is to take place, it must be a decision of choice, not a decision brought about either by default or by the continuing domination of an abuser over a child. Valerie Howarth, Director of ChildLine, once described sexual abuse as dramatically reducing the options for a child. We need to ensure that our decision to rebuild a family means the child's options are increased, not reduced still further.

2. An overview

Jenny Still,
The Faithful Foundation

The subject of family rebuilding is extensive. This overview considers the subject from the perspectives of both sex offenders and their victims. It considers how our increasing knowledge of sex offenders can enhance and inform the work that we do with children and families, in terms of child protection, on-going therapy, long-term risk assessment and the possibility of family reconstruction.

Many families reject the offender; others are more ambivalent; some are determined to reunite. As we in the professional community begin to embrace the possibility of significant therapy for sex offenders, it follows that we also must build into our agendas the possibility of actively supporting families who wish to reunite. This requires a multi-agency approach to therapy, with those who focus on the offender having a working knowledge and understanding of the issues for children and families, and vice versa.

The content is drawn from clinical experience in working from child-focused agencies, followed by three years of intensive clinical experience with adult male sex offenders at the Gracewell Clinic in Birmingham.

What do we mean by rebuilding a family?

Rebuilding a family can take many forms and involve different situations. It may be either the offender or the child (or children) who left or was removed from the family home; there may have been abuse of a child still residing at home, or of a child who has since grown up and left; there may be an offender who wishes to return to his own family where his previous offending was outside the family, or a Schedule One offender now living with a new family where he wishes to stay.

'Partnership' with the client? – an historical perspective

Throughout the life of a case there is a series of potentially fraught child protection decisions to be made, relating to, for example:

- assessment of risk and safety;
- registration;
- possible legal action;
- removal of the child or children, or of the offender;
- choices for mothers;
- contact and the extent to which it should be supervised;
- where contact should take place and whether it should include overnight stays;
- whether the family should be reconstituted or not.

All such decisions may be within the context of the offender being:

- bailed, possibly with conditions;
- remanded in custody;
- serving a prison sentence;
- on probation;
- on parole;
- in treatment;
- in the community on no order and receiving no treatment.

Over the past ten to fifteen years the professional community has begun to acknowledge the seriousness of the problem and to make resources available to assist children and their families. But the relationship between professional and clients is often heavily conflict ridden and not the 'partnership' to which recent child care legislation refers.

Our work takes place in a context of many questions which are often difficult to answer. Why don't victims tell and, if they do, why do they not tell us everything? Why is interviewing them so difficult? Why do victims feel so guilty and responsible for their own abuse? Why can't some children get angry with their abusers but get so angry at their mothers? Do mothers know? Are mothers 'safe'? And, if the problem is as distressing as we know it to be, why do some victims/mothers/families say they want the offender back?

Historically, sex offenders have responded to detection, suspicion or disclosure with silence, denial or, at best, minimising their activities as reflected in the current low conviction rate. A common outcome of inter-agency child protection case conferences is that the child is believed but there is insufficient evidence with which to pursue a conviction of the alleged offender. In our interventions with children and adolescents who have been sexually abused we have had to develop our understanding and intervention strategies in a relative vacuum, away from the offender and from alternative sources, primarily the victim child and the child's family. We have been working with half information in investigation, prevention, treatment and in evaluating the risks of family reconstruction rather like doing a jigsaw with half the pieces missing. The offender has the information we need, but he has not been telling it to us.

As a result, in working with victims we have been limited to responding primarily to the effects and impact of the abuse that many victims experience; the symptoms of post-traumatic stress; and possible emotional, behavioural, sexual and relationship difficulties. We have looked to an understanding of family dynamics in terms of family background, relationships, interactions, the family's response to disclosure and to the victim and so on and at what needs to change for the situation to be safe for the future (Bentovim and others, 1988). Dysfunctional family patterns have been identified (Furniss, 1991; Bentovim, 1988) that are common among families that experience child sexual abuse; families that present as chaotic and enmeshed with confused role boundaries, or rigid, controlling and steeped in secrecy. This information is crucial and valid. It is what we see at referral: a snapshot of things as they are at that time. But there are two major difficulties. First the offender is conspicuous by his absence. Secondly, it does not account for **why** we see particular effects in any one individual child, nor the full picture as to **why** these family patterns are common to intrafamilial child sexual abuse, or even **what** it is exactly that we are protecting the child from. Do we, or the family, have real information on which to base a decision whether or not to have the offender in the home? **If he managed to conceal his activities before, how can we or they know whether or not he is doing it again?** The offender has remained the missing link.

How do sex offenders who abuse children do what they do?

Sex offending does not 'just happen'. It is self-reinforcing, addictive behaviour that the individual wants to do. The more he does it the more he wants to do it again and again, either to the same child, or different children, or both. But he must not allow himself to be caught. Therefore leaving it to 'just happen' is too risky. So he finds out what works and repeats it. He develops a cycle of offending behaviour which is planned, calculated and deliberate, moving from fantasy through to assault. He must control not only the child but the child's entire immediate environment.

There is no cure for illegal sexual arousal to children. Knowledge of his cycle is crucial to the offender, as the cornerstone to his learned self-control through therapy.

The implications of the offender's cycle for the victim and family

It is not possible in this overview to consider all the patterns of sex offending. This chapter focuses on basic, common components of offender behaviour and reinterprets them from the child and family perspectives, demonstrating how we may usefully use such information to overlay our existing understanding of victims and their families, and to enable the client family to have real information on which to base their own decisions about whether to reconstitute the family or not.

Stages of the cycle

Sexual arousal to children and pro-offending thinking

For some sex offenders their pro-offending thinking stems from the belief that children enjoy and, have the right to engage in, full sexual activity. Distorted thought and belief patterns develop accordingly. More common, however, is the sex offender who knows at one level that what he is doing is wrong. In that case, to be able to do it and live with himself he must make it feel 'normal' and permissible. He must convince himself that what he is doing is not really abuse. He must therefore also develop an entire system of distorted thinking, attitudes and beliefs which both supports his offending cycle and pervades his day-to-day behaviour.

He will seek to justify, minimise, excuse and deny his offending. 'I only did this ...'; 'I just did that ...'; 'You don't understand ...'; 'I only did it once ...'; 'It didn't do him/her any harm ...'. He will blame it on others, primarily the victim: 'He/she came to me ...'; 'He/she asked for it ...' – or the victim's mother who was 'never there ...'. An offender has to be egocentric to do what he does. His life focuses on 'Me ... Me ... I want ...' which is then superimposed on others: 'I want it ... so you must want it too ...'. If to him it is not assault, then it must be equal and consenting behaviour.

The ramifications for his victim(s) are considerable. These are not just words but symptomatic of broader attitudes, beliefs and behaviour, with the child on the receiving end at a time that can be crucial in his or her growth and development. Victims who exhibit a strong sense of personal guilt, blame and responsibility are reflecting the powerful transference and counter-transference process in this interaction. Whether or not a child is to be reunited with his or her abuser, knowledge of the particular nature of the process, individualised to the child, can make an important contribution in identifying that child's emotional, sexual and cognitive restructuring needs, as well as to assessment of future risk.

A trigger/excuse to offend

Some offenders do not perpetually sexually abuse children. They are able to have an active sexual relationship with an adult but appear to have an external trigger into offending. Stress, feeling low and an emotional and mental state of 'poor me' are often identified. But triggers that appear to 'just happen' are again more commonly deliberately contrived excuses to offend. For example, 'I offend because I drink' is really 'I drink so I can offend'.

This is a common process and adds a new dimension to understanding family dynamics as seen at referral. For example, a common trigger cited by offenders is family conflict, especially 'rows with my wife'. The question is, does that just happen or does he have to make it happen, to give him the right feelings to overcome his internal inhibitors? The excuse allows the internal voice saying 'No, don't do it' to switch to 'Yes, do it', and so to convince himself later when feeling guilty that it 'would not have happened if there had not been that row with my wife ...', and therefore that it was his wife's fault.

Fantasy

He will fantasise about what he wants to do sexually to the child. Fantasy acts as a comfort, a reinforcer, a disinhibitor and a rehearsal for future acts.

Targeting

Eventually fantasy will not be enough and there will be a need to put the fantasy into practice. He is unlikely to abuse just any child, that is too risky. He will therefore target a child who fits into his sexual arousal through, for example, appearance, physical build, dress, demeanour, personality. There has to be access and availability – that is, vulnerability – and a potential for being isolated away from friends or siblings; preferably a child with problems or specific needs that he can in some way fulfil.

Knowledge of the offender's past target group plus his current and possibly progressive fantasy is crucial in assessing future risk and avoiding false assumptions regarding potential future victims. We should not automatically believe the offender's claim, for example, that he would only abuse inside or outside his own family, or only stepchildren but not his natural children, or only boys but not girls, older but not younger children or vice versa, at least until this has been validated in his own therapy.

Grooming

Few offenders move directly into sexual assault: it is too dangerous. Preparations must be made. Grooming is the means by which the offender gains the child's 'compliance' or, in his distorted thinking, 'consent', and is the insurance to minimise the risk of the child telling, or being believed or heard. It is the trap. It is a crucial part of the offender's cycle. Grooming can last an hour, a day, weeks, months. In grooming, the child is potentially drawn even more into the offender's distorted thinking and begins to absorb it into his or her developmental learning process especially if a child is repeatedly abused over a period of time. As such, it is potentially as damaging to the child as the sexual assault itself and could account for a great number of hitherto unexplained individual victim responses.

Examples of grooming tactics include:

- Gifts, bribes, treats, outings

Case example:
P described his grooming of an 11-year-old girl whom he sexually assaulted over 15 months as 'treats and a chat' – 10p and a can of drink. Further into treatment, P dropped his guard and 'treats and a chat with Uncle P' became 'pay-offs for sluts'. 'Mr Nice' grooming was dropped once the child was ensnared and his cycle short-circuited to fantasy–minimum grooming–assault, in which the offending behaviour became normalised, not only for him but also for the child. The child learns: 'I'm worth 10p, I'm a slut'.

- Emotional indispensability (common in intrafamilial abuse)

Case example:
T was sexually assaulted by her stepfather S over a long period of time. She was angry at the friend who disclosed on her behalf, and with social workers and police for separating her from her stepfather. In group, she could show no anger at her abuser. In therapy, S eventually described a use of physical force during assault, with his victim fighting back and anticipating full rape. So why did the victim respond as she did to disclosure?

In therapy, S described how prior to assault he had groomed T by using the knowledge that she missed her natural father. He made her his favourite in the family; befriended her; gave her his time, 'love' and attention; listened to her troubles; shared her interests and activities, and did them with her better than anyone else. A perfect relationship. T became increasingly emotionally dependent on him. When this scenario was in place he began to sexually assault her. In therapy, T was experiencing greater immediate trauma at the loss of the groomer than at the abuser.

- Play

Some sex offenders are fixated to children, both socially and sexually. They enjoy the grooming stage of their cycle as much, if not more, than the sexual assault. They often indulge in play activities which they enjoy as much as the child. They can make adorable and seductive companions, where abuse becomes inextricably interwoven with fun, pleasure, and a distorted notion of love and affection for the child as well as the offender.

Other offenders enjoy play but in a different mode, involving, for example, a more obvious heavy sense of power, coercion and/or humiliation. Other offenders don't much like children or enjoy their company – grooming is a necessary means to an end. A child is likely to be affected differently, depending on which kind of groomer he or she has experienced.

There are many different kinds of grooming. Language offers a further powerful means to put responsibility onto the child and imply choice, normality and consent: 'You like this ....'; 'You're enjoying this ...'; 'Daddies do this because they love their little girls, it's normal' (to a five-year-old, about inserting his penis into her mouth). Another possible tactic is the deliberate use and manipulation of issues relating to homophobia with boy victims and so on.

These and other forms of grooming operate on many subtle levels and are unlikely to be understood fully by the victim. Knowledge of grooming provided by offenders can help the familiar victim outcome of blurred boundaries between abusive and non-abusive behaviour become more understandable.

Case example:
Eleven-year-old N was abused by her father who set her up for pornographic photography sessions and indecently assaulted her. In her own therapy she insisted that she had not been abused and that she wanted her father home. In her father's therapy it became clear that he had groomed N by setting up the photography as normal 'dressing up play and dance'; photography was just his hobby, which he did along with his wife. The whole process was made to feel normal to the child. The contact sexual assault was not owned to by the father until much later in therapy. The child never referred to it of her own volition.

The influence of the offender's grooming can be long lasting, even after the departure of the offender from the scene. It is often the best groomed victim who says 'I want him back'.

Victims' mothers are groomed too. The need for safe mothers should not be minimised but, again, this must be put in the context of the offender and how he operated. Assessment of risk often focuses on the non-abusing partner and whether or not she knew of the abuse at the time. In a vacuum it can sound hostile and accusatory, and it can lead to inappropriate negative conclusions regarding child protection and 'unsafe' mothers.

Sex offenders tell us in therapy that, if they are to abuse a child but not get caught, they must first isolate the child from anyone who may otherwise protect him or her, or whom he or she might tell, most importantly, the child's mother. An offender cannot allow for a mother and victim child to develop a close relationship; again, it is too risky. Sex offenders groom mothers as much as they do the child. Again, there is an infinite number of ways of doing this: ensuring the mother goes out at set times, to work or to socialise; undermining her as a parent; having sexual intercourse with her on the same day as sexually assaulting the child; setting up the child as a liar, promiscuous or as 'trouble' to the mother; and more.

Much current therapy and family reconstruction work focuses on the need to strengthen the victim–mother relationship and to facilitate a more focal power position for the mother within the family. But this cannot really be achieved without knowing how the offender manipulated her into a position of powerlessness in the first place. Without this information, such intervention strategies potentially place the mother in an even worse position and collude with the offender by placing the onus of responsibility (for his past offending and for future family change) on her while the power and control still lies elsewhere, unidentified, with the offender.

There are vital issues here for marital therapy which can provide a more realistic foundation to later family therapy, if family members so wish. **From the Gracewell experience, it is also the point at which many partners change their mind about family reconstruction.**

An assessment as to the viability or otherwise of family reconstruction must necessarily also include an evaluation of the family and what needs to change. It is crucial that the scenario that previously 'supported' the sex offending does not recur. Again, this can most helpfully be done within the context of the offender's cycle and how the family came to be that way, remembering that for the offender to offend and not to be caught, he must have controlled the whole surrounding environment.

Case example:
H raped his daughter B regularly from the age of 11 to 14 years. B was the eldest of six children. H groomed his wife out of the way by relegating her to a support service within the household, with himself as the purveyor of both love and discipline. He made her out to be vulnerable, helpless and not able to cope should the child disclose. He set up the target child as his favourite, who was in turn therefore envied, and eventually disliked, by her siblings. He then set up sibling conflicts with her as the focus, from which he then rescued her. He 'asked' to 'have sex with her'. She said no, so he continued to set up the conflicts but withdrew his support. The child was isolated within a hostile family with no support, which after a while she could no longer tolerate. She went to her father and said 'yes' to sex, he said 'no'. The pattern continued. She went back to her father and said 'Please have sex with me' – and he did.

This adds a new dimension to our understanding of family patterns, which again do not entirely 'just happen', and offers a vital additional component in the identification of what needs to change within the family.

The influence of the offender's grooming can be long lasting, even after the departure of the offender from the scene. **It is often the best groomed victim/partner/family who says, 'I/we want him back'.**

Assault

We are aware of the traumatising effect of sexual assault on a child but to what extent do we currently address in therapy what the offender did to the child? We are wary of exacerbating the pain and re-abusing the child by unnecessarily reliving the abuse beyond the necessities of investigation. But we now know from offenders how during assault they distance themselves from the child, do not pick up the child's affection and misinterpret the child's behaviour to suit their own ends. Fear, rigidity and tears become sexual arousal and desire. Often they do not even see the child; he or she becomes like a rag doll, a stuffed dummy. The child is deprived of a sense of self.

Before we consider supporting family reconstitution, we must establish whether we have adequately addressed the implications of these issues for the child, if he or she is in the home or in regular contact with the home. Do we appreciate the level of fear, bewilderment and confusion the child experienced and may still be experiencing when in contact with their abuser? How is this still interacting with the grooming they also experienced?

Conclusions

This overview has attempted to highlight the basic issues, focusing on key components of offender behaviour. The following conclusions may be drawn.

- Knowledge of the offender's cycle and distorted thinking can provide:
    - the foundation for therapy for the offender through which he may achieve learned self-control (not cure) and a viable means of assessing the immediate and long-term risk of further offending;
    - an understanding of the child's whole abusive experience, as a basis for even more individually focused therapy according to the child's specific needs, including appropriate cognitive restructuring;
    - a vital additional agenda for work with the mother/non-abusing parent in freeing her from any inappropriate sense of guilt and responsibility, and a greater assurance that therapy does not inadvertently collude with her powerlessness;
    - hard information for the family on which to base their decision whether or not to have him back, or keep him in the family, rather than the distorted information previously given by the offender;
    - hard information for professionals in different agencies on which to base child protection work, risk assessment,

    on-going therapy with victims and families and to evaluate the possibility of family reconstruction;
  - an additional perspective from which to assess what must change in the family.
- This can only be achieved through long-term inter-agency cooperation that goes beyond investigation into therapy, within a common language and a common structural framework.
- It must be presented as a mutually complementary service that makes overall sense to the family unit, as well as to individuals within the family.
- Family reconstruction should not be considered unless the offender has received therapy and demonstrated a capacity for appropriate change.
- There are undeniable resource implications in terms of professional time and skills. The possibility of family reconstruction where the family so wishes would need to be built into the therapy programme from day one. It should become a matter for step-by-step review, subject to the progress of all parties. There is no point in waiting until the offender is at the end of his therapy before deciding whether it is an option or not. Whatever the outcome, everyone in the family will need therapeutic time to come to terms with it, to accept or reject it in a way that permits a positive experience. The need for both therapy and monitoring would continue after reconstruction.
- Experience at The Gracewell Clinic suggests that it is possible for a case to have a positive and safe outcome and then to be closed. With some families the use of extensive resources in this way may be a good investment. But if we do not have the resources, should we proceed, and how? Who is family rebuilding for and why is it being sought?
- Knowledge of the offender offers a new level of understanding of the role a victim child may play in the bid for family reconstruction: as scapegoat, rescuer or sacrifice. Has this been addressed in therapy?

Children do have the right to their say but we should continue to remember that it is often the best groomed victim (or mother or family), who will say 'I want him back'. We must remember that children also have the right not to be the continuing mouthpiece of the offender.

3. Issues for and about children

Abe Glaser, Consultant Child Psychiatrist
Guy's Hospital, London

The scenario which family reconstitution within child sexual abuse might conjure up is one in which a child discloses to her mother that she has been sexually abused by her father; the mother embraces the daughter, comforts her and confronts the father who owns up to the abuse and takes full responsibility, begs for forgiveness, offers to and moves out, seeking and accepting treatment. No prosecution, or at least no custodial sentence follows, mother and daughter receive separate group therapy and, following a period of family work, the family reunites.

Even such scenarios, which might be considered to hold the best outcome, are riven with emotional pain. In any case, every aspect outlined is, although desirable, not always attainable and, as a proportion of the actual case histories of child sexual abuse, the picture presented is a fiction rather than a reality. As with other aspects of sexual abuse, with family reconstitution the interplay between the different factors is far more varied and complex. Issues **about** the child might be considered in terms of the child's needs, while issues **for** the child concern the child's likely feelings and responses.

The child's needs

Although these needs are by now familiar to most workers in the field, they probably merit reiteration whenever a new step in a sexually abused child's life is contemplated, since the possibility of their fulfilment may determine the likelihood or otherwise of the new step succeeding.

Following disclosure and thereafter, the child needs to be believed. Both for the child's safety from further sexual abuse and, equally importantly, for the child's emotional recovery, this belief needs to be held and expressed to the child by his or her primary carer(s). Ideally, although it is not always attainable, this belief should extend to the full facts of the abuse.

Many children feel themselves to blame for the abuse or at least for their self-perceived failure in not stopping it sooner. Some children will be blamed for disclosing or 'lying'. Before a family can be reconstituted, freedom from such blame needs to be ensured.

One of the key elements in children's emotional survival is the capacity to be able to talk about the abuse. Children therefore need to know to whom, in a new setting, they can talk at their will, both about the abuse and about some of their feelings. In practice, this is often difficult to ensure.

Having been abused, the child's sexuality needs to be especially safeguarded. Faced with the possibility of once again living with their abuser, this becomes particularly important. There is a question about the degree to which a previously sexualised relationship can be desexualised when the two persons return to live under the same roof.

Finally, the child needs to know the extent to which the abuser has been able to take full responsibility for the abuse and what treatment he has received. It would be expected that both would have taken place prior to rehabilitation. In practice, some degree of denial often remains.

The child's feelings

Before the child's feelings can be meaningfully considered, some questions require clarification. The term 'rebuilding' means the putting together of an entity previously taken apart. In the present context, this implies that someone had previously left the family, which is now to be reunited. This person may be the abuser or the child or children. The abuser may be the father, stepfather, adolescent son, possibly a grandparent or another member of the extended family previously living in the family. The question therefore arises: who is being returned, and where have they been in the meantime?

A further, related question is: who is the prime instigator for rebuilding a family or who most strongly wishes it? Is it the child, the non-abusing carer or the abuser? Or might it be professionals involved with the family? Indeed, when rehabilitation comes to be regarded as a successful outcome measure of professional intervention, this could have an influence on the decision to rebuild families. One might also wonder whether, from the child's point of view, there is always a choice in the matter.

These questions are posed without offering definitive answers since they will vary with each family. For instance, a child may feel guilt-ridden about a father's imprisonment and, therefore, duty bound not to oppose his return or to express misgivings; or the parents of an abused child might wish for the return of their adolescent son who had abused his younger sibling. However, in the context of rebuilding, the child's responses are the result of the interaction between the answers to these questions and the child's own feelings in relation to the pre-abuse, peri-abuse and post-abuse circumstances.

From the child's point of view, the nature of the relationship with the non-abusing carer is particularly important in the pre-abuse phase. Many abusers 'target' children whom they perceive to be unprotected, unlikely to disclose and emotionally vulnerable – all of which are related to the nature of the care the children are receiving. At the time of considering the return home of an abused child or the return of an abuser, this carer/child relationship will again come under scrutiny and, potentially, under strain.

The non-sexual aspects of the relationship between the child and the abuser during the abuse often continue to prevail in the child's mind when meeting with the abuser subsequently, especially after a period of separation. For instance, despite the presence of several protective and fully trusted adults, some children are frightened by meeting their abusing fathers. In somewhat less safe situations, where the degree of belief and support are less certain, some older children and adolescents construct quite elaborate plans to avoid close proximity to their abuser. This becomes more difficult once the two are permanently reunited. For other children, the ambivalence which they feel towards their abuser may become intolerable as they grow older, and when the physical distance between them narrows. In this context, it has also often been observed that, over time, children's feelings towards the abuser change. Some children who are initially very protective of him, gradually become more hostile and angry. Only a few later attain a more settled emotional state in which they are able to tolerate positive feelings alongside the full acknowledgement of their abuser's wrongdoing.

In the post-abuse phase, the nature of the relationship between the carer and the abuser assumes central importance. The closer this relationship is, the more difficult and compromised the child's position is likely to be. The clearest example of this seen with children who retract their allegation, often in order to safeguard this relationship, be it between parents and son or mother and cohabitee. In these situations, courts sometimes return children home for lack of proof and in the presence of ample denial of, and disbelief in, the abuse. For these children, the cost of this form of reconstitution of the family is retraction, or, put more starkly, living a lie.

Experience of continuing professional contact with families over some years is showing that, with the passage of time, it becomes more difficult for those young children whose families did not believe them fully at the time of the return home of abuser or child, to sustain the fact of the abuse as a past reality. Some slide into forgetting, others adopt a more outright retraction.

Most children would wish to be able to return to the care of their natural family. This wish is, to some extent, informed by the pre-separation experiences not directly related to the sexual abuse. It is also strongly influenced by the nature of the alternative care offered to the child, including the number of moves to which the child may be subjected. It is more difficult to determine to what extent it is the abused children's wish that their abusers rejoin them, or whether they feel in some way duty bound or protective towards their family in acquiescing to their return. For many, supervised and regular contact would suffice until they feel mature and secure enough to re-establish an independent relationship with the abuser.

There are some children who feel genuinely confident in their own or their carers' ability to protect them, and who feel believed and supported in their families. For these children reconstitution is the hoped-for and appropriate outcome. For others, while it may be hoped for it is, sadly, probably not appropriate. Longer follow-up studies are required to test this assumption. Meanwhile, the child needs to know what the definitive plans are.

Finally, two thoughts. First, in a society in which parental and family breakup is so very readily accepted, and in the light of the many painful feelings precipitated by child sexual abuse, one might ask: rebuilding at what cost and for whom? Secondly, does rebuilding require forgiveness by the child and is this possible?

4. The offender's perspective

Dawn Fisher, Forensic Clinical Psychologist
Raeside Clinic, Birmingham

In addressing the question of rehabilitating a sexual offender back into a family a number of issues need to be considered. There is often a wide gulf between what it is realistic to undertake, given limited resources and perhaps limited cooperation from the family concerned, and what the professionals involved regard as necessary requirements to be achieved. Frequently there are competing demands and conflict between what families want and what professionals consider to be in their best interests. Thus it is vital that those involved in family rebuilding have a clear understanding of the factors and issues to be considered so that they can use the available resources most effectively.

Likelihood of re-offending

The obvious question that is asked when deciding whether or not to attempt rehabilitation is the likelihood of the particular offender re-offending. From the offender's point of view, being allowed to live in a family situation is dependent upon being able to convince the professionals involved that there is no possibility of re-offending. Unfortunately, in trying to do this, offenders tend to deny the very things that professionals see as signs of progress. Offenders may believe that being truthful about their offending may cause professionals to view them as more dangerous, may cause their partners to reject them, and some may be denying the truth to themselves. Therefore they frequently respond by denying and minimising their behaviour and placing the blame elsewhere. Denial can be evident to varying extents; from total denial of the facts to denial of certain facts in order to lessen the severity, frequency and duration of the offending. Denial of certain aspects of the offending, such as prior thoughts and fantasies and planning of the offence, are commonplace. Another tactic is to deny any sexual component of the behaviour and to place the blame elsewhere such as on other people, other non-sexual problems, or the effects of illicit substances such as drugs and alcohol. An added factor when working with families may be that the distorted thinking, denial, minimisation and blaming may not just be a feature of the offender but of other family members as well. Thus rebuilding a family can often seem to be an impossible task, particularly when it is considered that the families that want to be reunited are often those viewed most suspiciously by the professionals involved. The reality, however is that there are a number of families which will go to great efforts to be reunited. Owen and Steele (1991) followed up 43 incest offenders released from a prison treatment programme. Of those offenders who were married, 34 per cent returned to live with their partners and 28 per cent were living with children. Overall, 63 per cent of the offenders were living with a woman and 41 per cent of those also with children. Given that rebuilding is a real issue for a number of families, professionals cannot ignore this aspect and need to draw on as many sources of information as possible in order to make informed decisions. Given the unreliability of offenders' self-reports, a thorough assessment will need to be based on a variety of sources of information. As each source of information is likely to have associated problems, assessments should not be based on a single source of information; rather, information from all the available sources should be considered as a whole.

Sources of information

Information from other offenders
One source of information is knowledge about other offenders, such as the known re-offending rates of categories of sex offenders. However, reoffence statistics are fraught with difficulty and thus can be very misleading. It is widely acknowledged that official statistics are an underestimate of the true extent of sexual offending. Victim surveys and self-reports of offenders reveal that only a small percentage of offences are reported and, of those, only a minority are convicted. Russell (1984) estimated that less than ten per cent of sexual assaults are reported to the police and less than one per cent result in the arrest, conviction and imprisonment of the offender. Russell further found that in her 1984 study only two per cent of incest cases and six per cent of extra-familial cases had been reported.

A further difficulty with offence records is that they can be very misleading about the **types** of offences that are being committed. This is due to offenders only admitting to a lesser charge and the difficulties of proving a more serious charge leading to that further charge being dropped. Another problem is that offenders may have committed many offences but are only charged with a few specimen offences.

Although studies indicate that different categories of sex offenders have different recidivism rates (incest offenders 4 – 10 per cent, rapists 7 – 35 per cent, non-familial child molesters 10 – 29 per cent against females and 13 – 40 per cent against boys, exhibitionists 41 – 71 per cent), it may be that certain types of offences are more or less likely to be reported than others. In particular, it can be understood how difficult it is for a child within a family in which there has already been a disclosure to disclose, knowing the consequences of doing so. Another issue to consider is the possibility that the particular offender being dealt with has committed other types of sexual offences. Abel and others (1988) found that 49 per cent of the incest offenders in their study had abused extra-familial children and 18 per cent of them had raped adult women. It can, therefore, be very misleading to label a sex offender as belonging to a particular category of offender. Furthermore, the position with regard to sexual offences records is less than satisfactory: studies which report on undefined populations of sex offenders can be misleading because they are lumping together offenders with varying recidivism rates and averaging across them, while studies which report on specific categories of offenders can be misleading due to their containing offenders who may have, in addition committed other types of sexual offences.

A further issue concerns the length of follow-up over which recidivism data is collected. Studies typically show that the longer the follow-up period, the higher the recidivism rate. This is particularly pertinent in the case of incest offenders as there is evidence of generational abuse which would only be detected with an equivalent follow-up period. Finally, reoffence statistics give a general picture but clinical practice is based on the individual and so there is a further difficulty of knowing how much of the general picture can be applied to an individual case.

Risk factors

Another source of information that is used to decide on likelihood of reoffending is the presence or absence of particular factors which are thought to be related to recidivism. Unfortunately there are few studies which have investigated the predictive value of such factors and so information is limited. A further difficulty is that the findings are generally based on small samples and so the generalisability of the data is questionable. Abel and others, (1988) found that there were five pre-treatment factors which predicted failure to complete treatment. Molesting both boys and girls was a factor that correctly classified 83.7 per cent of the sample. The other factors were: failing to accept increased communication with adults as a goal of treatment, committing both contact and non-contact offences, being divorced, and molesting both within and outside of the family. Surprisingly, the number of prior offences was not a predictive factor in the treated group, although it is often held to be highly predictive of recidivism in untreated offenders. Marshall and Barbaree (1990) reported that, for their sample, genital to genital/anal contact was the most predictive factor of reoffending. Owen and Steele (1991) looked at recidivism rates in incest offenders specifically and found that 6.8 per cent of those who completed treatment reoffended, compared to 25 per cent of those who did not complete treatment. They identified four factors that predicted reoffending: living in a different household from the victim, chemical dependency problems, offending against multiple victims prior to first incarceration and being introverted at the time of release from prison. Owen and Steele hypothesise that the introversion finding has implications for treatment as, in order for group therapy to be effective, there has to be some bonding between group members. Such bonding is particularly important for the development of empathy. Those individuals who remain reserved, detached, critical and aloof do not become part of the group and are therefore unaffected by it. The introversion measure may prove to be a highly useful tool for measuring change and merits further investigation.

Information from the offender

Despite the problems of unreliability of offender self-reports, there is still much useful information that can be gleaned from the offender. Use of skilled interviewing strategies can help to minimise denial and elicit the cognitive distortions and fantasies the offender may have, in addition to ascertaining the offender's attitude to the offending behaviour. Questionnaires are often criticised for their transparency which can result in offenders answering in what they consider to be a socially acceptable way regardless of their true beliefs. However, use of 'faking good' and 'lie' scales and more carefully constructed questionnaires can minimise this difficulty. In addition, requiring offenders to explain the reasoning behind their answers can be very revealing of their true attitudes. Much information can be gained from observing the behaviour of the offender in a variety of situations. If the offender is resident at a hostel or in prison, the staff's observations of the offender's behaviour over prolonged periods may be very revealing: ranging from observations of how the offender relates to others, to what sort of pictures they have in their room. The use of exercises such as role-plays and written exercises, such as a victim apology letter can provide information about offenders that they may otherwise have been able to keep hidden. The other source of information from offenders is that obtained from direct physiological measurement. The penile plethysmograph is used to measure sexual arousal and a measure of galvanic skin response is generally used to measure anxiety as a lie detector. Physiological measurement tends to be very controversial because of the problems associated with each of the methods, both in their administration and the interpretation of the results. The results of studies using the penile plethysmograph have proved controversial, with different studies finding differing results. Such studies have been criticised for using small samples and thus making it unsafe to generalise. Regarding the studies concerning arousal patterns in incest offenders, Quinsey and others (1979) found that they showed an appropriate arousal pattern whereas Abel and others (1981) found that their sample did show sexual arousal to children. Marshall and others (1986), however, reported that their sample were not so much aroused to children as unaroused to adults. Although this is not the place to review the literature on penile plethysmography, it must be borne in mind when interpreting the results of such an assessment that the relationship between deviant arousal patterns and resultant deviant behaviour remains little understood.

Information from other sources
The statement of the victim remains one of the most useful sources of information concerning the details of the offence, particularly given the offender's tendency to deny or minimise. However,

victims may also minimise due to difficulty in talking about what happened and so their statements can also be understatements of what actually happened. If there have been a number of offences, it is useful to collect as many of the statements as possible. The cooperation of the offender may be required in gaining access to statements in some cases. Relatives and friends of the offender may provide information, but the fact that they may have been groomed in what to say, or be too frightened to tell the truth, must be borne in mind. Finally, other professionals involved with the case, either currently or previously, may provide much valuable information. Given that different professionals often tend to work with specific family members, close liaison between professionals is vital when addressing family rebuilding.

Preconditions for rebuilding a family

There is a high degree of consensus among professionals about the areas that treatment should be focused upon and what the indicators are that signal a lessening of risk in the future, although they are yet to be empirically tested as being directly related to recidivism. Ideally an offender would be expected to have achieved the desired criteria as a prerequisite to rebuilding a family. However, it is acknowledged that offenders and their families are not always cooperative and, as the requirements of the professionals are often in direct opposition to what offenders and their families are willing to undertake, achieving all the desired criteria may not be a realistic aim. The goals to be achieved are as follows:

- Admit the full extent of the abuse. Obviously it can never be known what the full extent really is and so an account that is consistent with the victim statement is generally aimed for.
- Take full responsibility for offending rather than attempting to place the blame elsewhere.
- Demonstrate genuine empathy for the victim.
- Demonstrate remorse for the offence.
- Recognise and be able to challenge cognitive distortions.
- Demonstrate an understanding of their motivation to offend.
- Be able to admit to deviant thoughts and fantasies and to have developed appropriate control strategies.
- Be able to describe the situations which would pose a risk in the future.
- Have developed appropriate relapse prevention strategies.
- Acknowledge that there could be a risk of reoffending and

therefore realise that the offending behaviour can only be controlled rather than said to be cured.
- Improve communication skills in order to promote better relationships with others.
- Discuss the offending with the family as part of marital or family work.
- Develop a support network in the community of people who will act as monitors. The use of grandparents as monitors was reported by Wolfe (1990) as greatly reducing the risk of recidivism.

Sibling incest

When family reconstitution is discussed it is generally assumed that the offender is an adult. However, it must be acknowledged that the most prevalent form of abuse is between siblings. O'Brien (1991) compared incest offenders to non-incest offenders in a group of 170 adolescent sex offenders and found that the incest offenders had typically committed the largest number of offences, had been committing them for a much longer duration, and were more likely to have committed more serious offences and to have more than two victims. These results can probably be explained by the ready availability of victims to incest offenders. However, O'Brien further reported that the incest offenders were less likely to be court-ordered for treatment than the non-incest offenders, suggesting that despite their serious offending behaviour they were not viewed as seriously as they should have been. Given the prevalence of sibling abuse it is likely that professionals will be faced with the issue of whether or not to rebuild a family in which sibling abuse has occurred. It is vital that such cases are considered seriously and that the issues that apply in the case of the adult offender are not overlooked.

Conclusions

Although rebuilding a family may seem an impossible task, with professionals often having to work with resistant families and lack of resources, the reality is that it is an issue that cannot be ignored. It is therefore important that professionals do their best but, at the same time, acknowledge the difficulty of the situation. Professionals need to work together in an integrated way to develop better working practices, share information and develop support networks. Further research is needed to gather more data which will help identify those offenders who are most likely to reoffend, and to develop treatment techniques which will prove effective with this group. If we do not attempt to work with the high risk offenders then we are simply leaving the most dangerous offenders with the least intervention, rather than finding more effective methods of working with them.

5. Issues for and about the non-abusing parent

Jacqui Sayers, Social worker
Child and Family Psychiatry, Bath

This chapter considers the purpose and role of therapeutic work with the non-abusing parent in cases of disclosed sexual abuse, in the context of reconstructing or rebuilding families after sexual abuse. The chapter refers to a situation in which the non-abusing parent is the mother, the abuse has taken place within the family that is, the perpetrator of the abuse is a close relative of the abused child and the perpetrator is male. These are the circumstances of the vast majority of families with whom we work and where, after disclosure of abuse, there may be potential for work aimed at rebuilding.

In general, experience of working with families from minority ethnic groups is limited. While many of the issues for these families following disclosure of abuse will be similar, there will be the additional stresses of working and living within a culture and system that, at best, lacks understanding of the needs of minority groups and, at worst, is itself abusive of the power it commands over them (Mtezuka, 1989/90).

This chapter covers three key issues. The first, relating directly to the main theme of the book, considers reconstitution as one of a range of options. The second concerns how we understand the ability of the nonabusing parent to protect, and the third considers the importance of enabling therapeutic parenting by the non-abusing parent.

Rebuilding a family as one of a range of options

There is a tendency for professionals to refer to families as either working towards rebuilding or not doing so. From the early stages of our involvement, we are looking to clarify whether this mother is going to choose the perpetrator or her child. If she expresses a wish to have both then we are beginning the process of assessing the potential for successful rebuilding. If on the other hand she says she does not want further contact with the perpetrator, we can work with her towards independence and no contact. Along with colleagues, I am concerned at the extent to which we all polarise the situation for ourselves and for families from the beginning of our contact. In so doing, we shut out many rich and varied options involving contact between a perpetrator and other family members which stop short of fully rebuilding the family.

Our understanding of, and work with, families should be viewed not as an attempt to decide on whether or not a family can live together again, but rather as an opportunity to look at the extent to which the achievement of certain goals and tasks can open up a range of options for contact between the child, or other family members, and the perpetrator. This moves us away from an idea that we are either 'hopeful' or 'doubtful' (Bentovim and others, 1988) about a family's chances of reuniting. Instead, our exploration of the presence or absence of certain factors, and the resolution of particular issues enables us to consider different options for contact. Rather than thinking about what needs to be achieved in order for family members to live, unsupervised, under the same roof, we can consider what the possibilities for contact are following the successful completion of certain pieces of work.

The model that we use in this approach to the work resembles a collection of cogwheels, rather than a continuum with 'separation' at one end and 'reintegration' at the other. If we use the cogwheels model, we are constantly considering how movement and change in one part of the system affects movement and change in another. As work progresses and change takes place it becomes possible to look at the range of options for contact between family members, rather than considering how far the family has moved along a line towards the ultimate goal of reconstitution.

Consideration of any option involving unsupervised contact between children and offenders means that one of the most important areas on which we need to focus is the ability of the mother to protect her children from further abuse. Work with families following sexual abuse is complex and demanding whether or not we are considering options involving contact between child and perpetrator. All the areas of work discussed here are necessary and relevant in their own right. Working on these issues with the mothers in families can also help us in our assessment of a family's readiness for contact, if that is the chosen option.

How we understand the non-abusing parent's ability to protect

In order to work on this we need to understand, with the mother, what the process has been by which the perpetrator has managed to place himself between the mother and her child. In this situation a mother has been disabled from fulfilling her role as primary protector. Gerrilyn Smith, in a forthcoming work, represents this diagrammatically (Figure 5.1).

Figure 5.1 The network of potential abusers and potential protectors surrounding a child (Gerrilyn Smith, 1991)

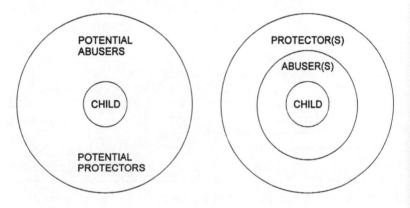

The diagram shows how the network of people around any child is made up of potential abusers and potential protectors. In a situation where abuse has occurred the perpetrator has placed himself in closer proximity to the child than the protective adults in the network. The aim of work with the protective adults becomes to reinstate them in closer proximity to the child, for them to show themselves as clearly as possible to the child as the protectors they are. For a mother to state an intention to bring a perpetrator into the family at some stage represents an enormous challenge to workers and family members in addressing issues of protection for the child. So what helps us to understand the ability of the mother to protect? There are five important areas upon which to focus our attention:

- belief about the abuse;
- taking the abuse seriously;
- taking action to protect;
- cooperating with the agencies;
- relationships with partners, extended family, friends and professionals.

Belief about the abuse

It would not be surprising if, upon first hearing that a child has disclosed sexual abuse a parent experienced a degree of disbelief. This would be likely to be greater when the alleged offender is in a close relationship with the non-abusing parent. Not being believed and not having adults take appropriate action are what adults, who experienced abuse as children, describe as having a significant, adverse effect on their experience of disclosure. It is also the reason that children most often give for not disclosing: the fear that they won't be believed (Kelly and others, 1990). In fact, research findings (Sirles and Franke, 1989) show that the majority of mothers do believe that their children have been abused.

When we are working with families looking at the potential for contact between offender and child it is particularly important to consider the extent to which the child has experienced support and belief by the non-abusing parent. Has the mother been able to validate the child's experience by saying that she believes that the abuse took place, and that the perpetrator of that abuse is the person identified by the child? Have there been any previous attempts by the child to disclose that have been ignored by the mother? If so, what is it that has made it possible for the mother to hear her child this time?

Taking the abuse seriously

Believing that sexual abuse took place, and acknowledging the seriousness and impact of it are distinct and equally important. A mother may believe her child but fail to take the abuse seriously. Signs that she has taken it seriously include listening to what the child says about the impact of the experience, acknowledging the distress and pain for the child, placing responsibility for the abuse clearly with the adults involved, and taking all possible steps to ensure that the child is safe from further abuse by the same, or a different, perpetrator.

Taking action to protect
When a child discloses abuse, the protection of the child becomes the priority for all professionals involved. We must consider whether or not a mother is able adequately to protect her child from the perpetrator and other possible abusers. Initially, the separation of the child and offender is imperative. The difficulty for the mother, who at this point makes a choice between her child or the perpetrator, is clear. The clarity with which this decision is made, and the extent to which she is able to maintain it, is helpful in understanding the mother's ability to protect. If she can demonstrate from the outset a total commitment to the separation of her child from the offender and take all possible steps to keep them apart (while that is necessary), then she shows that she understands the risk to her child of further contact with the perpetrator. These choices are, however, harsh and her need for support and encouragement in making them does not, in itself, minimise commitment to them.

Cooperating with the agencies
When we make plans at case conferences and agree on courses of action that are in the best interests of the child, we do not necessarily expect that parents will agree, but we do need parental cooperation with the plan. It is important to make a distinction between co-operation and compliance. Our understanding of a mother's ability to protect is helped by considering carefully the extent to which she has taken seriously the child protection requirements of the agencies involved. However, we need to think carefully about the extent to which the demands of the agencies on the mother are realistic. It would, for example, be unrealistic to expect that a mother could protect her child from the perpetrator who creates opportunities for contact with the child outside the home. We must ask ourselves whether the demands for protection that we make of the mother could be met by anyone, whatever their relationship with the child or however determined they are to ensure the child's safety and protection.

Relationships
One of the significant, secondary effects on the family of disclosed sexual abuse is that the mother becomes a lone parent. At a time when she most needs support and help, she is likely to be struggling

on her own, caring for and helping children who have complex needs. We have to consider not only the impact on them of the abuse of their child or children by a trusted partner or close relative, but the economic and social impact on them of separation, imprisonment of the perpetrator, stigma and isolation. We also know that many mothers in these families will have a personal history of abuse, and unresolved issues relating to the previous, possibly undisclosed, abuse will be re-stimulated by the discovery of the abuse of their child. In this situation, many unsupported women look to replace the partner who has left. It is essential to work with mothers to understand the extent to which their new relationships afford protection for the children in the family. This is not only important in relation to partners but also members of the extended family, friends and professionals. What are the supportive structures that are in place to assist the mother in the task of protecting her children while she attempts to rebuild her own life?

Our next concern must be to enable therapeutic parenting, and the importance of this in relation to keeping children safe within their families.

How we enable therapeutic parenting

We often overlook the potential for parents who are protective to offer their children therapeutic, healing help in addition to adequately protecting them, although we understand this concept well in relation to foster carers. We expect foster carers to develop skills, as parent figures, that will facilitate a therapeutic relationship with the children in their care. A variety of groups and training courses for foster carers help them to meet the needs of sexually abused children placed with them. Similarly, we should be considering the therapeutic potential of the relationship between children and protective parents. The mother is primarily responsible for the protection of the children in the family, knows the children best, is likely to remain their main carer, and has lived with them through this trauma. Furthermore, many mothers of children who have experienced abuse have also been abused themselves and have the potential to understand very well the therapeutic needs of their child.

It is unrealistic to assume that short term, direct, professional therapeutic input to the child following the disclosure of abuse, would be sufficient to meet the child's needs in the longer term. Many workers will have the experience of children returning for help some years after the initial phase of work with them and their families has ended. As children pass through different developmental stages, so they understand the abuse in different ways. The way in which their lives are affected by the abuse changes, and they are likely to need help to address the different issues raised at each stage of their development. If we enable mothers to develop their potential to offer therapeutic parenting, then they will tend to be better equipped to address the therapeutic needs of their children in the longer term. There are a number of ways in which this may be achieved.

Considering impact issues

For a mother to understand and help her child with the impact of sexual abuse, she needs knowledge about the ways in which children are affected by their experiences. It is likely that many of the impact issues for the child are also issues for the non-abusing parent: fear of further abuse of the child or other children in the family, guilt, anger with offender and possibly child, depression and low self-esteem. Suzanne Sgroi (1982) identified ten impact issues in her *Handbook of Clinical Intervention*. We need to help mothers to see that these issues are significant for them and for their child. Drawing on this in our work with mothers can enable them to help their child deal with the impact of the abuse.

For most children it will be more important that they are understood by their mother than by a professional. The mother is the person to whom the child is likely to keep returning to work through the impact of the abuse.

Educating

Professionals have access to a wide range of age-appropriate books, worksheets, colouring and play materials to facilitate the task of communicating with children about their experiences, helping them to express their fears and worries and working with them on issues of self-protection and safety. If we are to ask mothers to complement our work and continue it, or indeed to take on the tasks instead, then we need to provide them with access to these materials too. We may work jointly with mothers and children to begin this process which can continue long after professional therapeutic involvement with the family has ended.

Encouraging openness and communication
In situations where abuse has taken place in a family, a distance between mothers and children has been created by the perpetrator. Had it been possible for mother and child to have open and honest communication, then the offender would not have been able to achieve satisfactory closeness with the child for grooming to begin and abuse to develop. It is critical, therefore, that we work with mothers and children towards establishing openness and trust. The development of such a relationship will create an atmosphere in the family in which it is possible for healing to happen through talking, and will increase the chance that any future abuse would be disclosed at an early stage.

Conclusion

This chapter presents a framework for professionals to address issues for and about non-abusing parents in their role as primary protectors and caretakers of their children. The assumption has been made that work with non-abusing parents is vital, irrespective of any decision regarding reconstitution. Rebuilding is no longer the sole focus of intervention but is considered as one among a range of possible outcomes.

Those who work with families following sexual abuse disclosure must view the non-abusing parent both as an essential resource in any aspect of the family and individual work and as someone who is likely to be needful of all help that can be offered. It is often stated that, at the very least, we should be concentrating our therapeutic and protective efforts on the child victim. I suggest that unless we view mothers not only as primary protectors but also as potential therapists for their children, and assist them all the way in this task, then we are ignoring a massive resource. We may have paid too much attention to what are identified as the weaknesses in mothers in abusive families and given insufficient acknowledgement to strengths and potential.

We should remember, too, that it is not the task of the mother to demonstrate to professionals that the perpetrator can be trusted to return to live with the family and not reoffend. Dawn Fisher, in chapter 4, considers issues for and about the offender, and it is important to note that focusing on the mother, the non-abusing parent, and her ability to protect, should not minimise the significance and importance of work with others in the system.

Neither does it minimise the responsibility of the offender either for the offences or for work towards change.

There is also a need for work with the child, to assist him or her in the task of learning self-protection strategies, but research suggests that this 'last line of defence' (Finkelhor 1984) is not very effective against the determined and skilful perpetrator (Kelly and others). The most effective area of impact then remains that of working with the known protectors to strengthen them in this role.

6. Deciding to rebuild a family after sexual abuse

Margaret Adcock
Social work teacher and consultant

The authors of previous chapters have discussed the issues that need to be considered in relation to the child, the non-abusing parent and the abuser before a decision is taken to rebuild the family. Translating these into the process of making actual decisions raises a series of questions for professionals. These are:

- What are the aims of rebuilding the family?
- What is the context and why is this decision being taken now?
- What are the criteria for a decision?
- How should all the relevant material be put together?
- What work will be required?
- The use of statutory orders;
- Who will be involved and how will they work together?

In this chapter each of these questions is briefly considered.

The aims

It is helpful first of all to establish the long-term aims and goals for the family. The answers to the other questions may then be considered in terms of how they would contribute to the achievement of these long-term goals. Without goals, professionals and families may find it difficult to resist the pressures that will come from many quarters throughout the decision making and any subsequent process of rebuilding, and to monitor whether the decision to rebuilding remains the right one.

The writers in this book and other professionals in the field agree that the goals of rebuilding the family must include the prevention of further abuse, and promote the well-being of the victim, other children and the non-abusing parent. The second goal should include preventing the victim subsequently becoming an abuser. These goals need to be shared openly and explicitly with the family and other professionals and their agreement to pursue them should be sought formally. This will contribute to the establishment of an appropriate context for decision making and subsequent work with all members of the family.

The context

There needs to be recognition that the professional and the family context will be influenced by many factors. It is clear that ever since the existence of child sexual abuse first became widely publicised, the government, the courts, local authorities and the general public have been dismayed by the consequences of disclosure and have been looking for some 'sign of hope': an indication of potentially positive outcomes in at least some cases. Children themselves have poignantly expressed the wish that families need not be permanently disrupted or broken asunder as a result of their disclosure. Many adults have echoed this sentiment and recently the courts have begun to weigh up the relative harms of disrupting the family or exposing the child to the risks of possible future abuse.

The idea that it may be possible to rebuild the family after abuse is likely to induce hope in many people. It will be very popular and may lead to considerable pressure to attempt rebuilding in many cases. The situation may be likened to that of a terminally ill patient and his or her family who clutch at any straw, however slender. Children who are unhappy in care, mothers who miss their partners, parents who want their children back, social workers who cannot find suitable placements may all create an impetus for rebuilding. The fact that there is as yet little data on the situations in which rebuilding may be successful, or on long-term follow up may be ignored. For example, Bentovim and others (1988) state that about 14 per cent of families in their project were reunited. Meinig and Bonner (1990) in Seattle give a figure of 33 per cent. Fisher, in chapter 4, quotes a slightly higher figure.

Fashions can be created very quickly in child care when interesting new ideas are developed which make the work seem rewarding for families and professionals, and create viable alternatives in stuck situations such as a shortage of appropriate placements. If, in addition, new developments seem not only to be cost-effective but also to offer financial savings, there is likely to be very great pressure to introduce them on a large scale. The swing from residential care to fostering in the later 1970s and 80s is an example of this.

Philosophically, the notion of rebuilding families after sexual abuse would seem to tie in well with many of the concepts underlying the Children Act 1989. Section 1(6) (the check list) introduces the notion of weighing up children's needs, looking for the least detrimental alternative, and not making an order unless it can be shown to be better for the child. Care is now thought to be damaging for many children; good placements are in very short supply; there is a risk of further abuse in care and families are thought to be the best place in which to bring up children. All these ideas could create pressure for rebuilding. At the same time, however, they may lead to a minimisation of existing or future harm to a child. It is worth remembering the apt comment of Glaser, at the seminar which preceded this book, that the best of knowledge about what to do gets distorted by the reality of the cases, and the shortage of resources and expertise.

The criteria

Whatever the pressures for action, professionals and families need to think through beforehand what would be involved in any change. Sayer has stressed the need to consider a range of options for contact rather than only looking at a decision about rebuilding. If the goals are the prevention of further abuse and the promotion of the wellbeing of the child, the child's wishes and feelings clearly need to be ascertained before a decision is made. Glaser has outlined the dilemmas that may exist for the child and asks: 'rebuilding at what cost and for whom?'

Initially, professionals and family members need to consider the criteria both for decision making and for expectations of the family lifestyle after rebuilding. Written criteria have many advantages. They provide an explicit, visible structure for families and professionals. They offer each family member information about expectations. Family members read and re-read them and reflect and can, if they wish, talk to each other away from the professionals. Written criteria are more likely to be perceived as having a universal applicability rather than being a personal message to an individual family. This can give some family members confidence and enable them to express their wishes and views to the professionals, which in turn may help to reduce feelings of persecution by the professionals. During the process, some family members who were originally in favour of rebuilding may change their mind.

Each team or programme will want to develop their own criteria. Examples from American projects (*Violence Update*, Oct 1990) include the following:

Returning the treated sex offender to the family

- Children have a right to refuse to live with a child molester.
- Child molesters will be seen as a continued threat to children even after therapy.
- Child molesters cannot have equal co-parenting rights with non-abusing parents.
- The non-abusing parent makes all the decisions regarding the children (the abusing parent can provide suggestions but not make final decisions).
- The abusing parent acknowledges blame and does not project this on the victim.
- The reintegration process can take from one to three years.
- The family will participate in all recommended treatment modalities (individual, group, family and marital work).
- A worker never works in isolation.

Server and Jansen (1982) suggest that expectations for life in a rebuilt family may include the following ground rules:

- The child says he/she will get help if they are approached again.
- The abusing parent cannot be alone with the children.
- The abuser will not enter the children's bedroom or bathroom without a chaperon present.
- The offender is not to initiate physical contact with children.
- The offender is not to be involved in the physical hygiene of the children.

The rationale for developing criteria is to achieve the long-term goals of protecting the children and promoting their long-term well being. These are not ordinary children. They are children with special needs, who require a form of family life designed to meet those needs. The comparison is not with ordinary 'good enough' families but with adoptive and foster families. Adoptive and foster parents are provided with education and training, and assessed formally for their suitability. They have to demonstrate awareness of their children's special needs and to pay attention to the way their family life is structured and organised. Parents in rebuilt families need the same awareness of their children's needs and a willingness to structure their lives and behaviour in certain ways. They will need the same careful and repeated explanation, discussion and education.

Assembling the relevant material

Assessment is the basis of all good decision making and planning (Department of Health 1989). A good assessment involves the family in the process from the outset so that, as far as possible, parents and children contribute to and share the professionals' developing understanding of what may need to change. From the outset, consideration needs to be given to the possibility of rebuilding at some later stage. The purpose of this is not to raise false hopes or fears in family members but to ensure that everybody is clear about what would need to happen. Department of Health (1991) *Working Together* 5.17.5 states that the child protection plan should recognise that the abuser might want to return home after a prison sentence and should make a statement about what would happen in this event. This kind of forethought should also, in my view, apply to any situation where the abuser or the child is away from the home when the original planning is done.

The multidisciplinary team will need to be clear and agree about the purpose of assessment. Assessment is often understood differently by different professions. Workers who have been involved with individual family members need to share their information in order to assemble a comprehensive assessment of the strengths and weaknesses of the family as a whole, and their ability to meet the needs of the children (see Department of Health (1988) *Protecting Children*). At the point of rebuilding, the assessment of a child's needs should include considerations of the long-term consequences of abuse for the child. Assessment should also detail what intervention or treatment is required and the anticipated process of change, including the relevance of any statutory orders which would be relevant to the changed situation (see below). Writers in the earlier chapters have delineated many of the areas that need to be covered, including the non-abusing parent's ability to believe what has happened in the past and to work towards protecting the children in the future.

What work is required

It will be difficult to involve families in the process of thinking through the implications of rebuilding if the professionals are perceived as being resistant to the possibility of any change in the present situation. An initial willingness to explore different options, however impossible they may seem, may make cooperation with families much easier. A subsequent decision not to proceed, if this is required, may then seem more comprehensible and more acceptable.

The writers in the earlier chapters have made quite clear the extent of the work which is required with all members of the family. The style of work involved requires detailed discussions about the offence and its effects, sexual behaviour, family rules and relationships, and confrontation about any contravention of an agreement. The worker will need to help family members discuss such issues as the patterns of the offender's abusive behaviour; how he arranged time alone with the victim and how secretiveness was maintained. The worker needs also to be able to help family members to recognise possible warning signs in the offender's behaviour and to establish clear behavioural responses to these signs. These behaviours must have been practised in family sessions at home. This style of working may be unfamiliar to workers trained primarily in a psycho dynamic model. They are likely to require further training and support to undertake such work.

Good supervision in this work will be absolutely essential. Workers will be operating in a stressful situation where there will be a great deal of anxiety, weighing up of risks, and, often, unfamiliarity with the work. They need an opportunity to talk with someone who is aware of the agency's responsibility and who can take a somewhat more detached but informed view of what is happening. If the manager is not skilled in this area, it may be necessary for a local authority to have a consultant as well.

The use of statutory orders

The multidisciplinary team will need to consider the statutory basis of their work. Morrison (1991) has shown that the research indicates that some families and individuals are more likely to be able to engage in treatment where there is an order. He quotes Sgroi (1982) who said 'the track record in persuading perpetrators of sexual abuse to undergo voluntary therapy is abysmal. Perpetrators rarely remain in an effective treatment programme when the pressure to participate slackens.'

Even if an offender is already in treatment under an order, the team also needs to consider the position of the child. If the offender has been away from home, the child's name may not have been on the Child Protection Register, and there may therefore be no protection plan. There may not be a Care Order or a Supervision Order. Following rebuilding the position may be very different, and issues in relation to both the register and potential proceedings need to be reconsidered. There may well now be a significant risk of likely future harm and either registration or some kind of an order may be helpful. If a court order is sought the court would require a clear explanation of what benefits the order would bring. A case conference to discuss this could be helpful for both the child, family and professionals.

If the family is of a different ethnicity or culture from the professional, a great deal of care will be necessary to ensure that the family's customs and modes of operating are understood and are acknowledged in any rules that are set about the way the family should behave. It will also be important to ascertain whether the family understands what they are being asked to do. Language and different customs may make comprehension difficult particularly around areas of intimate personal and family life. A recent newspaper article described a patient who complained about stomach pain. He was asked by his doctor whether he had noticed blood in his stools. He said 'No'. The doctor did not know that in this man's culture one did not say 'I do not know', nor that it was taboo to look at one's stools.

Overall, rebuilding will require a considerable investment of time, skills and resources in a family. Professional reliability and continuity will be very important. This may be very difficult to achieve in the current economic situation. Providing this service on a large scale would require a very considerable input from local authority social workers. It is questionable how possible this is at a time of cuts in public spending and of reorganisation, and a purchaser–provider model which appears to recognise little place for treatment within the local authority service and relies on buying-in from health authorities and voluntary agencies.

Who will be involved in the team and how they will work together.

It is essential that a lead agency is identified which will take responsibility for pursuing the long-term goals of protecting the children, and ensuring that decisions made and work undertaken facilitate these goals. Because of their statutory child protection responsibilities, it is likely that this agency will, in most instances, be the local authority even if a social worker is not undertaking detailed work with the family. Other professionals must be prepared to accept the lead role of the designated agency. Dawn Fisher remarked that professional conflicts often arise when there are problems in the family and that the offender's therapist may then be scapegoated by other professionals. The lead agency should be able to help other professionals retain their focus on the child when there are disagreements or conflicts among them.

To facilitate good interdisciplinary cooperation, Trowell suggests that the professionals initially need to decide what each of their roles are and who will undertake which areas of work. Clarity about this will help to keep the work on course when pressures mount both within and outside the family. It can also help the team, at an early stage, to identify and reduce misunderstandings and hidden differences of meaning attached to terms like supervision, which, if undetected, could lead to disagreement and conflict later on.

The chair at meetings needs to have the capacity to help the professionals share and evaluate the information they have and to enable them to reflect on the process of their work. These are tasks that require both managerial and professional skills, as well as an ability to stand slightly outside the process and take an overview.

Conclusion

Rebuilding a family is a complex process, as both step-families and families with a child returning from care have demonstrated. Children often find it hard to adapt to the new situations and relationships. Their behaviour may be difficult and testing, placing considerable strains on the family's capacity to function. When rebuilding occurs after sexual abuse, there will be additional strains. Meinig and Bonner state that the process presents significant risks for both the family and the workers. It is therefore essential that professionals do not bow to pressure to compromise or make uninformed decisions and that their agencies provide them with every support in this difficult work.

Appendix: The workshop session: The practitioner's challenge

Anne Hollows, Child Abuse Training Unit
National Children's Bureau

This appendix is based on the reports from the workshop session of the conference on rebuilding families after sexual abuse. During the workshop session, groups of practitioners from different disciplines worked on a case study to try to establish what interventions would be required if the family were to be rebuilt. The guiding principles for any rebuilding were taken as being an effective reversal of the four preconditions of child sexual abuse developed by David Finkelhor (1984).

- A potential offender needed to have some motivation to abuse a child sexually.
- The potential offender had to overcome internal inhibitions against acting on that motivation.
- The potential offender had to overcome external impediments to committing sexual abuse.
- The potential offender or some other factor had to undermine or overcome a child's possible resistance to the sexual abuse.

Groups, which contained staff from a variety of disciplines but with a majority of social workers, were asked to highlight key areas for attention by Area Child Protection Committees including therapeutic resources, training, and agency management. One of the first points to emerge from the group workshops was the novelty of having a multidisciplinary discussion about the principles of rebuilding families. This concern highlighted for all of us the importance of establishing good multi-agency communication at practitioner level around the principles to be followed in cases of this kind as well as a clear management framework for this task. In this context, discussion of Finkelhor's four preconditions threw into sharp focus the need for practitioners from different agencies to understand the value base from which each was working and to define for each working group a common core to which they could all adhere.

It was felt by many to be unrealistic to contemplate a complete reversal of the preconditions and, in particular, that the motivation of the offender could be controlled but not reversed. It was agreed that whoever was working with the offender would have to undertake work around acknowledgement of the offender's sexual orientation and work towards identifying the factors which provoked a difficulty of control in this area. In respect of the motivation of the offender, it was also important to include the immediate family group and to seek extended family support for this task. The offender's partner would require a clear understanding of all the risks involved in order to support the offender's motivation positively.

Practitioners identified a clear need for therapeutic work on the response to internal inhibitors, which again would involve not only the offender, but the couple and wider family. The need for clear multidisciplinary communications was highlighted here: it was pointed out that when an issue is being worked upon in more than one arena, there need to be explicit statements of what can and what cannot be confidential, as well as a forum for coordination of activities.

The process of building external inhibitors was seen as quite critical. In this respect, one of the key tasks would be to strengthen the mother's position in the family. Practitioners felt that it was helpful to develop contractual arrangements with mothers about what was permitted in the family and this would be strengthened by group work, aimed at building protection skills, with the child who had been involved in the abuse as well as with siblings.

The urgent need for the development of therapeutic resources was highlighted in all the groups. Many of the participants at the conference came from areas where there were no formal channels for this work, and spoke of their own practice being limited by their skills and their experience as well as by a lack of supervisory experience in their agencies. In this context, work around denial or minimalisation of the offences and the risks was seen as a prerequisite for longer-term treatment. One group looked specifically at the tensions inherent in developing work around rebuilding. Tensions that were noted included the establishment of a hierarchy of needs whose therapeutic interests should be prioritised? There were also tensions in relation to timescale. It was clear that the jigsaw of therapeutic interventions needed to be very carefully constructed in order to ensure that, as far as possible, there were common goals and that activity with one family member did not militate against a separate activity with another family member. This concern also focused on the consideration of treatment styles where it was clear that a family member who was receiving help from more than one source could become quite confused by different approaches.

Alongside all of this, the issue of resources was seen as quite critical. One group asked the question, 'rebuilding at what price?'.

There were major concerns about situations where the final outcome might be less than or different to that desired by the family members. In this sense the work could be compared with some of the difficulties addressed by social workers counselling in terminal care cases where the eventual outcome was not going to be that which people wanted, but the process of the work undertaken might in itself contribute towards a greater acceptance of an unsatisfactory outcome. It was acknowledged that working towards imperfect outcomes posed major difficulties for all practitioners involved.

Critical to all the potential for work in this area were two factors: first, a clear multi-agency management framework for developing and supervising the work, for building resources, and developing and maintaining skills; second, a real cooperation over what these resources, whether physical or human, would involve. The potential for Area Child Protection Committees to address this issue was seen as critical to the difficult practical task of judging which resources to use in a particular case and how far to proceed towards a goal of rebuilding. There was considerable acknowledgement from the groups that the contributions of the speakers at the conference offered models for good practice. That this practice is widely unavailable at present, was indicated by the number of groups who incorporated into their plans for the case they were considering, referral to one or more of the specialists who had contributed to the conference. This led to an emerging sense of frustration that the work was almost beyond the grasp of many agencies. Not only were they being asked to undertake difficult work in a climate where often the best which could be achieved would be less than ideal, but they were faced with a lack of resources, a lack of skills and a lack of management commitment either within agencies or between them. This was balanced by an enthusiasm to try to change the situation. There was no doubt in the minds of many of the participants that this was work which should be on their agendas. The questions which the workshops were unable to address were how to get work-related issues and resources for the work onto managers' agendas. They were clear that multidisciplinary management commitment and support was the first step in developing this much-needed work.

References

Abel, G, Becher, J, Murphy, W and Flanagan, B (1981) *Identifying dangerous child molesters.*

Abel, G, Mittelman, M, Becher, J, Rathner, J and Rouleau, J (1988) 'Multiple paraphiliac diagnoses among sex offenders', *Bulletin of the American Academy of Psychiatry and the Law,* 16(2), 153 - 68

Adcock, M, White, R and Holmes, A B eds. *Significant Harm.* Significant Publications.

Bentovim, A, Elton, A, Hildebrand, J, Tranter, M and Vizard, E (1988) *Child Sexual Abuse Within the Family: Assessment and treatment.* Butterworth

Department of Health (1988) *Protecting Children: a guide to the comprehensive assessment of children and families.* HMSO

Department of Health (1989) *The Care of Children: Principles and Practice in Regulations and Guidance.* HMSO

Department of Health (1991) *Working Together Under the Children Act.* HMSO

Finkelhor, D (1984) *Child Sexual Abuse: new theory and research.* New York: Free Press

Furniss, T (1991) *The Multiprofessional Handbook of Child Sexual Abuse.* Routledge

Kelly, L, Burton, S, Regan, L (1990) *An Exploratory Study of the Prevalence of Sexual Abuse in a Sample of 16-21 Year Olds.* Child Abuse Studies Unit, Polytechnic of North London

Marshall, W L, Barbaree, H E, and Christophe, D (1986) 'Sexual offenders against female children: Sexual preferences for age of victims and type of behaviour'. *Canadian Journal of Behavioural Science,* 18, 424-39

Marshall, W L, and Barbaree, H E, (1990) 'Outcome of cognitive-behavioural treatment'. In Marshall, W L, Laws, D R, and Barbaree, H E, ed. *Handbook Of Sexual Assault.* New York, Plenum.

In Morrison, T, Erooga, M and Beckett, R (1994) *Sexual Offending Against Children.* Routledge

Morrison, T (1991) 'Change, control and the legal framework'.

REFERENCES

Mtezuka, M (1989/90) 'Towards a better understanding of child sexual abuse among Asian communities'. *Practice*, Autumn/Winter, 248-60

O'Brien, M J (1991) 'Taking sibling incest seriously'.

Owen, G, and Steele, N M (1991) 'Incest offenders after treatment'. In Patton, M Q ed. *Family Sexual Abuse*. Sage

Quinsey, V L, Chaplin, T C, and Carrigan, W F (1979) 'Sexual preferences among incestuous and non-incestuous child molesters', *Behaviour Therapy*, 6, 213-19

Russell, D (1984) 'The prevalence and seriousness of incestuous abuse: Stepfathers vs biological fathers', *Child Abuse and Neglect*, 8, 15-22

Server and Jansen (1982) 'Contraindications to reconstitution of sexually abused families' *Child Welfare* Vol 61 no 5

Sgroi, S (1982) *Handbook of Clinical Intervention in Child Sexual Abuse*. Lexington MA: Lexington Books.

Sirles, E and Franke, P (1989) 'Factors influencing mothers' reactions to intrafamily sexual abuse', *Child Abuse and Neglect Vol. 13*, 131-39

Smith, G *ed.* (forthcoming) Morrison, T 'Partner, parent, protector: conflicting role demands for mothers of sexually abused children'.

Stuart, R *ed.*, *Violent Behaviour: social learning approaches to prediction, management, and treatment*. New York: Brunner/Mazel

Wolfe, S (1990) paper presented at workshop, Birmingham

Index

A
abuser/victim relationships 10–13
abusers
  acceptance/denial of responsibility 6, 16–17, 20–21, 25, 31, 36, 40, 47
  addictive behaviour 1, 7–8
  characteristics of 2–3, 8–9, 23–26, 46–47
  observation of 24
  returning home 5, 17–20, 41
  transference of blame 21
addictive behaviour 1, 7–8
adolescent sex offenders 26
adoptive families 40–41
alternative care 19
  see also fostering
Area Child Protection Committees 46, 48
arousal patterns 24
assessment of families 13, 21, 41–42

B
belief in victim 6–7, 10, 12, 16–17, 19, 31–32, 42

C
Care Orders 43
carer/abuser relationships 18–19, 31
carer/victim relationships 18
case conferences 6, 32, 44, 46
case studies 10–13
change, maintenance of 2, 4, 13, 15, 42
chemical dependency 23
child abuse
  background 1
  media coverage 1, 38
  permitting circumstances 2, 12–13
  preconditions 46–47
child care legislation 7, 39
child protection 1–2, 5–7, 12, 14–15, 32, 40, 44
child protection plans 41
Child Protection Register 43
child care professionals *see* professionals
ChildLine 4
Children Act (1989) 39
children in care 38–39, 44
children's feelings 6, 13–14, 17–20
children's needs 2, 9, 14, 16–19, 39, 41
children's rights 2, 40
children's sexuality 8–9, 17
cognitive restructuring 14, 25
communication 26, 35
concealment 7
consenting behaviour 9
contact
  options for 29–30, 39, 42
  restoring 3, 17–29, 23

unsupervised 29–30, 32, 40
victim/abuser 6, 9, 32
conviction rates 6–7, 21–22
court orders 43
criteria, written 39–41
cycle of behaviour 8–14, 42

D
developmental stages 34
deviant behaviour 24
disclosure of abuse 6, 11, 13, 16–17, 22, 28, 33, 38
divorce 23

E
education after abuse 33–34
education of families 40–41
emotional ties 11
ethnic minority groups *see* minority ethnic groups
evidence of abuse 6–7
exhibitionists 22
extra-familial abuse 21–23

F
families
 adoptive 40–41
 assessment of 13, 21, 41–42
 education of 40–41
 rebuilding *see* rebuilding families
 working with 5, 35–45, 47–48
family patterns 1, 7, 9, 13
family therapy 13, 42, 48
family units 2–4, 15, 33, 38–39, 47
fantasies 9–10, 20, 23
fathers 17
financial implications 2, 39, 43–44, 48
Finkelhor, David 46
fostering 33, 39–41

G
generational abuse 22
'good enough' parenting 40
Gracewell Clinic 2, 5, 13, 15
grandparents 17, 26
grooming 1, 25
 of mothers 12, 15
 of victims 10–13, 15, 35
group therapy 16, 23
guilt 6

H
Handbook of Clinical Intervention 34
health authorities 44
homophobia 11
hostels 24
Howarth, Valerie 4

I
impact of abuse
 on mother 32–33
 on victim 7–8, 10, 13–14, 34, 41
imprisonment 18, 21, 33
incest 21–22, 24, 26
inter-agency cooperation 5–7, 15
 see also multi-disciplinary teams
intervention 3–4, 7, 12–13, 17–18, 27, 35, 41, 46
interviews 6, 23–24
introversion 23
isolation of victims 10, 12

L
language problems 43
legislation for child care 7
lie detection 24
local authorities 44
lone parents 32–33

INDEX

M
maintenance of change 2, 4, 13, 15, 42
male victims 11, 23
management of intervention 2–4, 48–49
marital therapy 13
minority ethnic groups 28, 43
monitoring 15
mother/victim relationship 12–13
mothers 2–3, 6, 9, 12, 14, 16, 28–36, 32, 47
   history of abuse 33
   new relationships 33
multi-disciplinary teams 41–49
   see also inter-agency cooperation

N
non-abusing carers 2, 17–18, 28–37, 42, 47
   ability to protect victim 3, 19, 28–36, 42
   therapy 15–16, 28–36

O
offence, types of 22

P
parental rights 40
'partnership' 6–7
penile plethysmographs 24
photography 12
physiological measurement 24
placements 38–39
pornography 12
prevention of future abuse 37, 39–41
primary carers *see* mothers
prison sentences 1, 21, 41
prisons 24

professionals 3–5, 14–15, 20, 25–28, 33–35, 37–45
Protecting Children 41
protection of children *see* child protection
protection skills 36, 47

Q
questionnaires 24

R
rape 22
re-offending 1, 21–25, 27
rebuilding families
   aims 37–38
   attitudes to 37–41
   motivation 5–6, 13, 17–18, 28–29
   rules 40
recidivism *see* re-offending
reconstructing families *see* rebuilding families
registration of families at risk 6, 43
rehabilitation of families *see* families, rebuilding
residential care 39
resources 15
restoration of contact 3, 17–20, 23
risk assessment 5–7, 14–15
risk factors 23
risk of future sexual abuse 1, 10, 16, 20–27, 38, 40

S
safety of children *see* child protection
Schedule One offenders 5
sentencing 1, 6
separation of victim/abuser 1, 5–6, 16, 32

sex offenders *see* abusers
sexual assault 13–14
Sgroi, Susanne 34
sibling incest 26
siblings 13, 17–18, 47
social workers 4, 11, 38, 43–44
   see also professionals
sons 17–18
statements of victims 24–25
statistics 21–22
statutory orders 41
stepfamilies 44
stepfathers 11, 17
Supervision Orders 43
support networks 26

T
targeting 10
teenagers 26
therapeutic parenting 3, 28, 33–34
therapists 44
   see also professionals

therapy
   abusers 5, 8, 12, 14–15, 40, 43
   non-abusing carers 15–16, 28–36
   victims 11, 15–16
treatment 21, 23, 26, 40
   abusers 1–2, 4, 41, 43–44
   victims 1, 16
triggers to offending 9

U
'unsafe' mothers 12

V
victims 5–15
   belief in 6–7, 10, 12, 16–17, 19, 31–32, 42
victims becoming abusers 38
Violence Update 40
voluntary agencies 44
voluntary therapy 43

W
Working Together 41
written criteria 39–41

Becoming a member . . .

The National Children's Bureau offers an extensive Library and Information Service – probably the largest child care information resource in the UK. We also run a comprehensive programme of conferences and seminars, and publish a wide range of books, leaflets and resource packs. In addition, the Bureau gives members the opportunity to tap into an influential network of professionals who care about children, helping to set the agenda for the nineties and beyond.

Membership of the National Children's Bureau provides you with:

- a quarterly mailing containing:
  – *Children UK*: the Bureau's journal
  – *Highlights*: briefing papers containing summaries of research findings and recent reports of legislation on relevant issues;
- access to the library and information service including databases, books, journals and periodicals;
- first access to the findings of our research and development projects;
- advance notice of our extensive programme of conferences and seminars throughout the country;
- **concessionary prices** and advance details for all Bureau publications;
- **concessionary prices** for all conferences.

The National Children's Bureau can support you in the day to day task of meeting the needs of children and young people. For further details please contact Jane Lewis, Membership Marketing Coordinator, National Children's Bureau, 8 Wakley Street, London EC1V 7QE or call **0171 843 6047** for further information.

National Children's Bureau Publications

Recent works include:

Day Nurseries at a Crossroads
Meeting the Challenge of Child Care in the Nineties

Developing a School Sex Education Policy: A positive strategy

Educating Disruptive Children
Placement and progress in residential special schools for pupils with emotional and behavioural difficulties

The Future Shape of Children's Services

Children and Residential Care in Europe

For further information or a catalogue please contact:
Book Sales, National Children's Bureau, 8 Wakley Street, London EC1V 7QE
Tel: 0171 843 6029   Fax: 0171 278 9512